I0749789

Poetry Nook

Volume 3
December 2013

Frank Watson, Editor
Tiara Winter-Schorr, Editor
Erny Herawaty, Contributing Editor

Published by Plum White Press LLC

For information concerning reprints, email:
followingtheblueflute@gmail.com

ISBN-13: 978-1939832061
ISBN-10: 1939832063
LCCN: 2013917427
BISAC: Poetry / Anthologies

Cover image by Jiri Hera, licensed via Shutterstock.com

Published in the United States of America

Submissions:

https://poetrynook.submittable.com/submit

Monthly Mailing List and Subscriptions:

http://www.followtheblueflute.com/p/poetry-nook-monthly.html

Also by Frank Watson

Poetry

Seas to Mulberries

Edited Volumes

The dVerse Anthology
One Hundred Leaves
Fragments

Table of Contents

Editors' Note

Welcome to the third issue of *Poetry Nook Magazine*. We are thrilled to present a feature with the mystical poet, Yahia Lababidi, and a photograph collection by Bobby Gutiérrez, a New Mexico-based photographer.

This issue is rich with philosophical meanderings and spiritual reflection. In these pages, you will also find a spread of art and poetry from regular contributors, such as gennepher, Bauke Kamstra, John Reinhardt, and Chris Smith. *Poetry Nook* is continuing to grow with the help of our readers and our writers, and we thank you all for your support.

As always, we encourage you to reach out to us with thoughts, suggestions, and feedback. Monthly subscriptions are now available at:
http://www.followtheblueflute.com/p/poetry-nook-monthly.html

We wish you an enchanted season of giving and thanks.

Frank Watson
Email: followingtheblueflute@gmail.com
Twitter: @FollowBlueFlute

Tiara Winter-Schorr
Email: winter.schorr@gmail.com
Twitter: @twinterschorr

$100 PRIZES

FOR POETRY AND ART

Congratulations to the winners of the October 2013 poetry and art prizes: 1stCitizenKane for poetry and Chris Tuarissa for photography. Each will receive a $100 prize. We have reprinted one piece each of their work on the following pages.

Next month we will announce the winners of the poetry and art prizes that appear in this month's issue. Both art and photography will be eligible for the art prize. Reader feedback will be an important element in awarding the prizes, so please leave your feedback in an Amazon review or send it to us directly at:

Frank Watson
Email: followingtheblueflute@gmail.com
Twitter: @FollowBlueFlute

Tiara Winter-Schorr
Email: winter.schorr@gmail.com
Twitter: @twinterschorr

This Young World

This young world, or am I old,
and this young world's warmth and hope,
or am I cold and crippled by fear,
but crutches are made of dreaming.

1stCitizenKane

Chris Tuarissa

Poetry Nook

Volume 3
December 2013

If You Can't Be Purely Free

If you can't be
purely free
(we are slaves
to something)

be a mystery
(ask the moon).

Bauke Kamstra

The Field Behind the Dying Father's House

I'm the thin yellow
that escapes the dry grass,
the left-over dream
haunting the afternoon.
I'm the stillness of goldenrod
in the ordinary day
before the storm cloud breaks
and the wide trees embrace
their shadows. I possess no gift
of perspective that will deceive your eye.
I am simple and flat, a reflection
of sun forgotten on the ground.
Hovering between the earth and sky,
I belong to neither: no green
can swallow me, no blue
can overwhelm my singular purpose.
I hold this fragile landscape together
until night falls and turns everything—
the luminous barn, the brooding
house—into a quiet symphony of black.
I know its slow melody by heart.

Linda Nemec Foster

Headlights

Headlights
like
headaches
flash
in my mirror.

Dave Read

There's a Jungle in My Mind

beez laine

Philly Automat

You've got to live, she told my sisters and me
as we dressed in crisp taffeta dresses
and *Capezio* black velvet shoes
embroidered with pink rosebuds
bought with money from my grandparents
who probably thought my mother bought bread
and eggs - not fancy shoes, but
she had her priorities   and one
was to treat her children to lunch
at Horn & Hardart's on Chestnut Street.

I'd approach the glass windows
with fists full of nickels and dimes, plunge
coins into slots; watch the doors pop open
to BLT sandwiches, macaroni & cheese,
coconut custard pie, rice pudding.

Year after year, my mother sat
like a 1940s film star,
her coffee without sugar, her ebony hair
pulled back tight in a shoulder-length ponytail,
a black piqué dress and marcasite initial pin
placed high on one shoulder.
She never ate during these lunches
(though she tasted from our plates);
and then, when ready, she'd open her purse
remove the gold lipstick brush
and redraw her lips in Spanish red
without a mirror, but with a steady hand.

Madeleine Beckman

Two Ravens

two ravens
how your wings
whispered
when my eyes
became stones

Debbie Strange

Final Arrangements

But there's no end to it. Ashes circulate. They breathe in urns
like virgins dreaming of a chance. The man tells me to sign here,
for a quick pick-up of my corpse that won't be cold for long,

once I slide into the flames. The end of shivering. The close

of silence, because on the other side, beyond the shore, there is
so much noise, all those people banging pipes on a railing, and
drunken laughter, people with smudged foreheads where a priest

marks their foreheads with mid-week. But if I burn, I burn. It

doesn't have to be quick. Pain just the idea of pain. The way
God comes and goes, a bored wraith, a wisp of light, you feel
nothing. What's the body but flammable dry leaves that collect

like pages of a book you haven't finished reading. Every *finis*

with a coda. Another page that almost blows across the lawn.
Yes, there's a community here, with regular trash collection,
roads to be plowed, children in school learning to spell your

name. Again. And again. And again. And again. And again.

John Allman

All

In the clearing of the stormy night
The strangest thing
Crickets are in the rain puddles
Stirring the stars.

Richard Moss

Do You Have Any Questions for the Pharmacist?

Wouldn't I in the old days be praying in
a field, the husks of now forgotten plants
scattered over me? The hiss of movement
among the trees only a doe followed by her
fawn? Won't this white circular tablet take
away my name? Isn't mindfulness like being
pressed to the earth, where I breathe deep
and long, where crows tango in the air, and
a chill sinks from my bones into a mothering
ground, as pity, fear and sorrow shape themselves
    into seeds that worry toward the sun?

John Allman

Blink

A photograph of graffiti art

Steve Baldwin

To an Anonymous Boy

Maybe I never knew his name
in three days— but I remember
a broken jeep, a hole in the floor
a pad in the back— we drove
out to the valley, dusty cotton
fields, straight dirt roads, no map.

It was 106°, we stopped to swim
in a ditch irrigating nearby grapes
its steep muddy sides held us
a moment gasping to climb out
we parked in a dark field overnight
must have made love, the boy shy
fumbling.

In the morning we found stale
donuts and orange juice, drove
some more past tall corn, potatoes,
thistles, hard white ground, air
conditioner broken, windshield
cracked, hot wind laying us back
in the dust, laughing nervously—
I barely looked at him, was he tall?

The hot valley breath sucked the air
from us, we were silent, staring at
miles of almond trees, tomatoes,
orange groves, aimless we wandered
in the sun waiting for another burning
night of more love, I forget his name,
if he had one, was his hair brown?

Mostly I remember the irrigation
ditch with steep slippery sides pushing
us back into the cold flowing water
choking we clawed up finally, lay
panting on the hot bank to dry, eyed
each other gratefully, not drowned.

Emily Strauss

Salmon Run

silver tips flicker
at the brush of noon

scaly sinew rises through
grizzly pawed & fish hooked waters

cool spawning pools
become scarlet paved

the open sea
empty-netted

Jane Mellor

Tea-Time with Babushka, Aged Ninety-Four

For Elisavietta Hartman Artamonoff

She described how she put the Tsarina at ease
at Kronstadt Fortress with kind English words,

the lapis lazuli in her chestnut curls,
and the splendid count on Nevsky Prospeck
years later in rags, who remembered,

She agreed Rasputin was opportunistic and odd
but not, surely, as bad as Saint Petersburg whispered,
and though a nation's fate should outweigh a mother's love
that, too, was understandable,

told how, in a Bolshevik jail, she was put in the cell
with the prostitutes, but resolved their fights
and they begged her to stay in *their* cell,
not be moved to the aristocrats' wing,

then she finished her tea, grasped her cane,
pulled herself up complaining as always
high time that she died; and she kissed
her great-grandson's jellybean hands, and left,

discussing Vietnam with the cabbie and God,
unaware that the gray plastic comb
had dropped from her hair.

Elisavietta Ritchie

Silvering Statues

silvering statues
on the dance floor of night
moonlight painted the garden
her gossamer gauze dress
shimmering

gennepher

Solitary Swan

solitary swan
circles as if lost, calls out
disconsolately

abyss/amiss –

unexpectedly
the river bends sharply, drops
into nothingness

Marianne Paul

At Midnight

... as though called from my bed / I stand outside

... midnight at my feet

... suspended between two maples a quarter moon / an owl somewhere along the river

Teresa Evangeline

Okinawa Park

Morning mist attaches itself
to these plains-
individual grass stems wet with dew,
drying later in the sunlit day.

My bike wheels encircle around
the Ryukyu Island, I watch puddles acting as tides
evaporating into masses of water vapor.

Naha is inscribed
with my daily tire patterns
etched with dirt, cut grass
and rice.

The rotation of my wheels cease
when clouds darken; I witness
ground geckos scurry trees

and these puddles that once carried
the weight of the Pacific Ocean,
now empty themselves
into the East China Sea.

Jamal Parker

An Earlier Autumn

... on a hillside below a silent barn / my grandfather wandered

... searched the moonlight for cattle long gone

... safe in an earlier autumn

Teresa Evangeline

With Our Pockets

With our pockets
full of sand dollars
we were
richer than ever
before or since.

Dave Read

Widow

It hurts to brush her hair
        anymore.
Mirrors are anathema to
black tangles
that choose where they
lie or fly,
with an occasional recommendation
from an uninspired
        hand.

Her eyes are flat,
        unblinking,
fix on what has left,
        negative space,
see invisible shadows,
        life stains,
in vague and familiar places –
        kitchen chair
        razor on the sink
        unmade bed –
that hold her gaze for

seconds, minutes, hours.

Nothing changes.

The fragrant, earthy garden
of her tended soil
in the long yesterday
will not bloom today.

She pushes a strand of hair aside.

Perhaps tomorrow
she'll empty his drawers
and closet.

Eusebeia Philos

He’ll Believe

He’ll believe
in the tooth
fairy
as long as she
keeps paying.

Dave Read

Change Is

Change is
our hardest
lesson
and what remains
in our pockets.

Dave Read

October cattails

October cattails
cling a little longer to summer's end—
Waiting blackbirds sing.

Leigh Herrick

Fruit

Meet me in the old grove
beneath the untended fruit
where the sun leaves
its last touch,
and we'll fill ourselves
of sweet flesh
in the warm grass.

Eusebeia Philos

A Sea of Crosses

a sea of crosses
blankets a field where he once
cried, and cries today

Michael Seese

Last Call

their mating dance
inside a bottle
reaches an inglorious ending
under bright lights and
open eyes

Michael Seese

Hitodama

Reading death poetry,
wondering what my last words
shall be.

Steve Shultz

Solitude

Like a painter in a harem...

which nude will he paint,
which side of himself express,
who is alone in this place?

There is a hole in the palace.
He digs.
The tunnel plunges to a maze
an ancient spider spinning his web
not a single fly in the catacomb of thread
gets trapped to fill his days...
        In the cold, subterranean wind
        the fabric of thought shivers and sways.

The spider is dead
at the centre of his spread.

....

Like a writer by a lake...

watching the reflection of himself;
there are two of me, he thinks
and both are all alone.

vipul rikhi

Black Crow Morning

... downstairs / harsh words

... grey pulls back the covers / crawls in beside me

... black crow morning falls on the meadow

Cletis L Stump

As If the Lies You Told Me

As if the lies you told me
were distant clouds
resting within
the impassive sky

Bill Ellsworth

Draining the Ocean

Darkness squirmed
above the
tumult of
flailing limbs.

Caresses deft
spilled light soft,
from the conjoined flesh,
over the brim.

Rivulets of light
tasted like the sea,
salty
and incipient of life.

The lapping sighs,
and the crashing waves
of guttural moans
unleashed an odorous strife.

In the redolence
of our entangled breaths
we discover, the pungent,
ancient ocean of creation.

Through our eyes
we drain it into
our memories
as an act of preservation.

Anupam Sinha

feather

i can't
remember you
yet i miss you
like a feather
maybe misses
its wing

Donna Falcone

Sanctuary

A Photography Collection by Bobby Gutiérrez

Bobby Gutiérrez is a Latino photographer and a life-long resident of New Mexico. His journey as a photographer began at the age of nine, when he discovered Polaroid cameras and began snapping photos of his surroundings. But it is in recent years that his interest developed into a focused passion.

His subject matter is centered primarily on religious sites unique to New Mexico and the Southwestern United States. Because he is an entirely self-taught photographer, he relies on his perception and intuition to capture images. When looking at his work, it is apparent that his natural gaze from behind the lens is what infuses his images with a sense of the sacred.

The following collection is centered on the idea of sanctuary: places of worship, respite and rest, and reverence. Some of these places are churches, some are monuments, but all offer the same notion of safety and comfort. All of the religious sites shown here depict a mixture of Catholic and indigenous heritage and are nested throughout the state of New Mexico.

We welcome you to "Sanctuary" and hope that you find the same enchantment and sacrality that we encountered in the photography of Bobby Gutiérrez.

Cathedral Basilica

Cathedral Basilica of St. Francis of Assisi, Santa Fe, NM

Santo Niño Chapel

Santo Niño de Atocha Chapel, Chimayó, NM

At Santuario de Chimayó

Virgin Mary at Santuario de Chimayó, Chimayó, NM

Santuario de Nuestra Señora

Santuario de Nuestra Señora de Guadalupe, Santa Fe, NM

The Hand of St. Francis

Tree trunk carving of the hand of St. Francis of Assisi, Santa Fe, NM

Mary in the Rose Garden

Virgin Mary in the Rose Garden at San Felipe de Neri Parish, Albuquerque, NM

Nuestra Señora de la Luz

Nuestra Señora de la Luz, Cañoncito, NM

The Nature of Belief

Dancing
in the wind
it could be
a samba
and though they said
it was a waltz
the tree
I believe
was never false

Da natureza de crer

Dançam
ao vento
balançam
podia até ser
samba
mas elas disseram
que era valsa
e eu acredito
não existe
árvore falsa

Fereh Rocha, translated from the Portuguese by Frank Watson

Ripeness

Night shadows stretch damp
dew-laden—full of autumn
and windfall sweetness

Jane Dougherty

Holidaying in Chimney Woods

These woods are like a mother
putting all embers out.
Sweet wind winnows me out of
all secret worries.
As I dip myself into the woody stream,
tension termites disappear.
Throats of birds broadcast unceasing songs
like our FM station.
When a tribesman squeezes a honey-comb, I
ride my tongue up the palm.
My mind convalesces slowly here
under the foliage.
Fireflies fly out through the windows
of my skull.
Fresh thoughts are cooked in the seclusion
of the woods.
Shoots of dreams reappear, breaking the dried
pods of my memory.
I see the fossils of a paradise, which we had lost
under the past.

Chimney Woods are in Kerala, India.

Fabiyas M V

Autumn Sky

Cold brilliance of starlight
the dark odour of damp earth
beneath the leaves

Jane Dougherty

Grape Harvest

Red leaves fall
the vine aflutter
with blackbirds

Jane Dougherty

Truth

Truth
You don't know
What you do
To me

Amie McIntyre

Memory Keepers

collecting stories
like the pages it creates
some fact, some fiction
each leaf holding memories
of the way things used to be

Kathryn Dyche Dechairo

Missing

A clean handkerchief
wraps around grief
like a soft breath
of frost
breathless in the
approaching face
of spring.

Your hand, my hand,
our fingers—
hiding from the memory
of touching
a shuttered moment—
reach into
our pockets
for handkerchiefs
that are not there.

Jessica Otto

Hope

from "Earth Cycle"

a house, stone drenched in salt,
windows to the rumble of a sea,
in the attic, a table, a chair

the front door, wedged open,
a fire glowing, begging the wind,
begging a stranger to sit, be warm

perhaps stay.

Valentine's Day

Laura Kynch

Moose Calling Moon

Women are bunched
in twos and threes.
Peeling pulp, soaking sweet grass,
threading porcupine quills.
Heads bowed, mouths pursed,
bending the flattened quills
zig-zag like a braid.

Rolling down
  the Finn Town Road
comes a muffled roar.
Heads lift—
  first one,
  then the others.

They watch
two white men
drive by
in a big bloated beat-up
Buick. 8-racked
redbrown buck strapped to the hood,
the long, graceful neck twisted
like rodeo steer.

Tires screech on the blacktop.
Metallica blares.
The Buick skids the turn,

squeals up the causeway.
The women smile.
Look at each other.

white men.

Michael Campagnoli

When I Was a Bell

When I was a bell
and you listened
all the way to the end

Roary Williams (Coyote Sings)

Chocolate Archaeology

from "Earth Cycle"

When this world ends, and
Icelandic ash-clouds descend,
future archaeologists will find me

encased in a dusting, sugar-white,
marshmallow bones wrapped around
a dark chocolate heart, gone liquid.

In ten thousand years
they will pour me out, and wonder
at the bitter-sweetness of life.

Laura Kynch

Birthday Toes

from "Earth Cycle"

Standing in the shower,
the safest place in the house
where no neighbour can hear
me choke, head bowed,
I count on my toes:

Paths taken, summits seen.
So what is it in me
that is so terrible?
Why do I still walk alone
on ten salt-splashed toes?

Laura Kynch

I Took a Ride

I took a ride
On Execution Road
Humming to beats
Playing in my bones
Searching the horizon
For the last exit
Home.

Chris Smith

I Disappeared

I disappeared
in the darkness
a place
with no words
and a graveyard
of feelings
around me

Chris Smith

Panoramic Ocean

We sit at this clothed table
where the land meets the sea

in a glass-enclosed room
nibbling on ocean fare

to the yelp of seals
weaving about the mouths

of hunter dolphins
and just before their very last gasp

I wonder who decided
on the perils of the food chain

and where it begins—
on the plate before me

or in the ocean's shimmer
blinding my green eyes.

Diana Raab

And Then, When

And then, when
I didn't expect it,
the piano next door
slow and soft
in the autumn's chill

M. Kei

Hence

when we lay side by side
covers tossed in array,
our eyes fall into a trance

where our giddiness
becomes beyond playful
and like erupted volcanoes

we become new humans
only wondering
when the next time will be for us.

Diana Raab

She Is a Study of Lines

She is a study of lines –

composing the movements that conduct her presence,
  like the waves of light and motion
sketching themselves on a tidal sea –

respecting not the contested borders of being, the
  lights and shadows of noon and night, but the
dawning of their grainy shores –

essaying the contrasts.

Brad Johnson

Garden path

Yesterday I followed
a garden path
to the end of the sky
you touched the day
you walked to the sun
on that path of rocks
that escapes my name
right now when you touch
the cold shoulder on your side
but also the one which wants you,
every waking night
when I am without you.

Diana Raab

I Can Speak Your Name

I can speak your name
like cherries on the tongue

& still I do not know you.

Bauke Kamstra

Cold Fruit

You used to tell me
that pomegranates were for children
seeds like blood bloomed
out of cat scratches
and teeth wiggled free
with the help of rock candy.

You used to cut them
only a little, so you
could feel them breaking
apart when you pulled
free the halves and exposed
the tiny red rubies of light.

You told me that winter
could last for years—
snow ice snow ice—
as long as I remembered
to crunch hard each seed
between the white of my teeth.

Chloe Clark

Climbing Hard

climbing hard
i follow an eagle
beyond the cliff
just for a moment
the sky inside me

Sandi Pray

Incision

It is said that the first
cut is painless
that the only thing felt
is the color of water rushing
past the eyes of sailors
drug deep in the clutches
of mermaids or krakens or
weights tied to feet
after the mutiny, after the storm.

It is told that the second
cut is the one to fear
that it feels of the day
after you let the dirt drizzle
through your fingertips and even more
it feels of when you washed
your hands later and mud
caked the basin and all,
all you could think
for hours for days for years
was of that mud and the way
it looked from certain
angles like a face.

Chloe Clark

Butterfly

Jasmine Pradissitto

Waiting for you

The hours line up like scars
To mar the passing of days
Burning into months
And aching into years.

Kayleigh Brookes

Waiting

waiting
in the shadows
what was left unsaid

gennepher

Into Stillness

Reach into stillness,
breathing lightly into a
world bathing in waves of heat.
The careless greenery shrugs
off its enthusiasm.
The world is dry, not brittle;
only a sun's consuming
power can shadow the earth's
youthful enthusiasm

still as midnight in winter,
but not asleep.

John Reinhart

Alchemy of the Saints

A photograph of graffiti art

Steve Baldwin

Always Raining

In my memory,
it is always raining –
hands pressed to glass,
your eyes say goodbye;
one drop slaloms
gently down your neck,
then disappears.

The water seeps
into my shoes
and I squeak all
the way home.

John Reinhart

I Took the Wind As My Lover

I took the wind as my lover
sowed tears into the earth
lost myself in the silence
until it left me
cold
on the inside.

Chris Smith

High Above

High above
the bowl of salt

that was once
a lake

the small shadow
of a hawk.

Bauke Kamstra

It’s the Lies

It’s the lies
you tell
yourself
I likely won’t
believe.

Dave Read

as a writer

as a writer
i appreciate

how you've
scripted

the events
between us

into your
own piece

of fiction

Dave Read

Closer

Ink Stitution

Interview with Yahia Lababidi

We are honored to interview Yahia Lababidi this month, author of the recently released collection of poems, Barely There, *which explore a variety of spiritual, meditative, natural, and other topics, in typically concise and impactful form. In this interview, he expands on the spiritual and philosophical development that led to his collection, as well as the "chrysalis" state of his current growth. We follow the interview with a brief selection of the poems included in his book, which we highly recommend reading.*

—Editors

In some poems, such as "What If" and "Embracing, We Let Go," you hint at a spiritual struggle or development. What has been your spiritual evolution over time? How has it influenced you as a person, in the choices you've made in life, and as a poet?

This is a big question, and I'm not sure such deep movements of the soul withstand being discussed directly, but I'll try. Yes, this new book is a document of a spiritual struggle or development, as you put it. For years, I worshipped at the altar of the mind, and now something stirs that is overthrowing the tyranny of the rational. In one of the poems in *Barely There*, called "Expedition," I sum it up this way:

> After decades of exploration,
> discovering I stand at the shore
> of intellectual knowledge
> before an infinite sea
> of the esoteric.

An alternative title for my book of short poems was *In Chrysalis* to suggest this transitional period that I'm undergoing. Also, there's another poem in this collection, "Kneeling in Stages," which serves as a kind of resume of my inner life and speaks of me better than I do myself.

So as not to sound needlessly elusive, I will add that I am a cultural Muslim, but was not raised as a practicing one. As a matter of fact, as a young man, I distanced myself from religion as a way of protesting against the type of religiosity that prevailed in my part of the world, and I generally did this through my readings in Existential philosophy. Only very recently, do I find myself fed up with the mind and its chew toys and returning to the mystical branch of Islam (Sufism) by way of Persian poetry and also the lives of (Christian) saints. I cannot really speak further of this evolution, since it is still occurring, but no doubt this force is reflected in my writing, as it is in the process of rewriting my soul.

In "Breath" you seem to find spirituality in nature. How do you think about nature in relation to you, and to humans in general?

There is a Persian mystic, Al-Ghazali, who describes well the spirituality found in nature, saying: "this visible world is a trace of that invisible one and the former follows the latter like a shadow." So, if there is consolation and inspiration in the natural world, it is because it mirrors the invisible world of the spirit and serves as a portal to access it.

What kind of relationship exists between creativity and spirituality, in your opinion?

Another fine, and vast, question. Creativity, as I understand it is amoral. It plucks its fruits from everywhere, without asking where they come from and what good they might be. Spirituality, perhaps, is about inhabiting a natural state of creativity, one that is more concerned with our moral development, and the revelation of the hidden relations between things.

Do you think there is a connection between poetry and prayer? How do they affect each other in your life?

I think of poetry as prayer. To write is to bow is to pray; bow so low and you kiss the sky. In fact, prior to this collection, I collaborated with a friend and fellow aphorist, Alex Stein, on a book of conversations called *The Artist as Mystic*. In this series of dialogues, we examine the spiritual dimension in the lives and work of thinkers and poets, such as Nietzsche, Rilke, Kierkegaard and Baudelaire.

We also see some influence from Eastern thought in "Exchanges," among other poems. How have you integrated different belief systems in your own life, whether religious or philosophical?

Western philosophy, my first love, is slowly being replaced by Eastern mysticism, Nietzsche by Rumi. Perhaps it is odd to say this but I see in Nietzsche a stunted Rumi. I am drawn to the captivating contradictions in both, the serious play, their radical ecstasy. But I see the example of scholar-become-poet, who then goes on to make of his life a work of art, more fully realized in the figure of Rumi.

In "Egypt," you talk of your "self-exile" yet the inevitability of remaining part of your cultural heritage. What prompted your "exile?" What are some of the ways your Egyptian heritage continues to influence you in daily life and as a poet?

I left Egypt nearly eight years ago because, quite frankly, I was gasping for air and it felt like something had to give. As it turned out, everyone else felt the same and that something was Revolution. What I did not realize was that, by being away, I was deepening my longing and appreciation for my culture. Also, as a result of the current upheavals, ex-pats such as myself find they naturally gravitate to the role of cultural ambassador or explicator, keen to communicate the Egypt we know and love, as we sift through the many distortions and contortions that are presented in both foreign and local presses.

What are your thoughts on the changes underway in

Egypt?

Difficult times. I maintain that the Revolution was absolutely necessary and recognize, ruefully, the revolution-fatigue I see setting in, where people are settling for the unsavory choices of Muslim brotherhood, or military rule, two faces of unfreedom. Yet, neither of these thought-dictators represent our uprising, nor do they offer a vision forward of unity, dignity or peace. I am heart-broken as I see how divided people are becoming and how they rationalize the senseless violence being committed. This is not the Egyptian character I remember and I hope during these trying times, when we are battling for our souls, we remember that *how* we fight for freedom determines *who* we become.

Your poetry does not have a lot of explicit political discussion, but there are some lighthearted reflections on issues like racism in "Skin" and commercialism in "Truth in Advertising." What do you think is the role of the poet in discussing societal and political issues or in keeping the art and the society separate?

I wrestle with this question on a regular basis. I think poorly digested politics make for bad art. At the same time, I think it unconscionable for the artist to fiddle while Rome burns, so to speak. Striking the right balance has been tricky, but I've found it easier to address issues of the day (politics, culture, etc...) in my prose, as the poetry I do not own.

For readers who might be interested in my prose meditations on the role of artists in times of political crises, or commentary on Egypt throughout the years, here are a couple links:

http://newint.org/contributors/yahia-lababidi/

http://n.pr/18Kbhsi

In "Hothouse" you talk about poets you cannot stand. What are your thoughts on the currents of contemporary poetry? What types do you like and dislike? What are you trying to accomplish as a poet?

I don't perhaps read as widely as I should when it comes to contemporary poetry, but the advantage of that is that I am always discovering new poets / poems I admire. (Here's a virtual library where I recite some favorites: https://soundcloud.com/yahia-lababidi). What I like in poetry is what I like in people: profundity, humor, attention to language. What I dislike in verse, similarly, is what I am not fond of in persons: superficiality, sentimentality and, in regards to language, a sort of gimmicky self-consciousness. What am I trying to accomplish as a poet? Goodness; to Be more fully, I suppose, and in some small way, perhaps help others also to do so.

What do you hope readers take away from your work? Do you aim to teach or to provoke thought in your audience?

I think in order to teach that cannot be your stated aim. But, I do believe in provocation, challenging assumptions and "telling the truth slant." I think it's not easy to speak to ourselves, and that we sometimes need to devise ruses. Poetry, at its finest can do this and bring us into contact with a larger reality. Then, if we're lucky, help us to transform, too.

Most of your poems are extremely brief. Do you think a shorter form has more impact? Do you think this is inherent in the concentrated intensity of shorter poems or do you think it reflects the changing tastes of contemporary readers as they have become accustomed to smaller bites of information?

All of the above.

To begin with, I'm an aphorist at heart and always try to whittle matters down to their essences. Further, the poems in this book were, to a large extent, inspired by the constraints of social media, specifically Twitter – so, I've found the 140 character limitation an invitation to create poetry in miniature. In this way, the poems in my new book are "barely there," on the page, the way their author is "barely there" off of it.

Who are your major poetic influences? We saw a quote from Rumi in your book and a reference to "the Way," which we assume to refer to Daoism. How have mystical poets influenced you? How about other types of poetry?

Yes, Rumi and the Persian poets exert a great influence on my being. Also, Rilke means a great deal to me; as he says "We are the bees of the invisible. We wildly collect the honey of the visible, to store it in the great golden hive of the invisible." Otherwise, Eliot was a formative influence and Rimbaud, and I still return to all the usual suspects who set me alight as a teenager. Spiritual tourist that I am, Daoism is also a source of inspiration as is Buddhism. If I had to pick a single book, at the intersection of poetry, philosophy and the sacred, it would be Lao-Tzu's *Tao Te Ching*. I regard it as inexhaustible and am struck anew by its fruitful paradoxes with each reading. Simply, I think it gets at the heart of life in ways that nothing else does.

What are your major non-poetic influences–whether people, other literature, events, etc.?

I think, if we pay attention, everything/everyone has something to teach us. Silence has been one of my greatest teachers; Solitude, too.

What are your plans for future work, whether in poetry or elsewhere in life?

After around a decade or so of aphoristic silence, I'm back to secreting these brief arts through the pores. In fact, I've a book's worth of meditations on art, morality, and spirit, and am taking my time to find the right publisher for such a project. Otherwise, I haven't a clue what comes next. More listening, deep self-diving for pearls.

Before we wrap up, we would like to give you a chance to speak to young poets who grapple with faith and writing. Madeleine L'Engle noted that when one is given a gift, one is obligated to serve that gift. Do you agree with this and do you think young poets should follow the idea that art is a type of service—either to be honest to their own potential, or to use what has been given to them?

Yes, I passionately believe that art is a calling and a life of service. In fact, this is the premise of my conversation: *The Prayer of Attention*

http://www.bu.edu/agni/interviews/online/2010/stein.html

My advice to young poets would be that, to honor the gift and be worthy of it, they must give of themselves, whole-heartedly, and hold nothing back. The more deeply you know yourself, the more you are able to truly reach others. The more fearlessly you share of your findings, the more likely you are to make an authentic connection with a stranger; in turn, liberating truths that are not just about you, or me, but us. Lastly, I would add that part of knowing ourselves entails working on ourselves - training the self and liberating the soul. So that we can answer Yes, when a winged poem approaches us and asks: Can I trust you? Is your heart pure to carry me, are your hands clean to pass me on?

Breath

Beneath the intricate network of noise
there's a still more persistent tapestry
woven of whispers, murmurs and chants

It's the heaving breath of the very earth
carrying along the prayer of all things:
trees, ants, stones, creeks and mountains alike

All giving silent thanks and remembrance
each moment, as a tug on a rosary bead
while we hurry past, heedless of the mysteries

And, yet, every secret *wants* to be told
every shy creature to approach and trust us
if we patiently listen, with all of our senses.

Yahia Lababidi

Gaze

A loving gaze is
sun, water, and soil
for a soul to grow.

Yahia Lababidi

Embracing, We Let Go

Perhaps, we are negotiating
not just with one, but always two
(who share the same soil, it is true)
one who lives, another who is dying

A shift in the balance begins to take place
once a love of silence is confessed
its roots run deep, its shade a world
and her fruits impossible to forget

From the first, we surrender something
and, gradually, consent to be emptied
seduced by so much soundless music
drunk and sated through lipless mouths

What use to name this silent master
preparing us for dying or the Divine
– I'm not sure there is a difference –
but know in embracing, we let go.

Yahia Lababidi

Meditation

Prayer is also anesthesia
so that we might cut deeper
and clean out our wounds.

When in doubt, meditate
upon your ancient ache.

Yahia Lababidi

Options

You can't bury pain
and not expect it
to grow roots.

But you can try
and tend tenderly
to its subtle fruits.

Yahia Lababidi

Skin

Funny thing, skin
how it can make you feel
like you belong
to another or the world.

With its distinct instincts
memory and desire
almost makes you wonder
who's wearing who?

Yahia Lababidi

Truth in Advertising

Morning epiphany
in haiku-like purity:
only freshly squeezed
separation is natural
shake well to enjoy!
In fructose veritas.

Yahia Lababidi

What If

If he truly believed in angels
they would appear, I said in a dream
(of whom I spoke I can't recall)

Then I remember disintegrating
into hot tears as I realized
that I also spoke of myself

And in that wild, greedy moment
I challenged an angel to appear
as I cowered in a darkened closet

Full of longing and terror, I endured
the suspense of that great What If
- relieved the angel did not answer.

Yahia Lababidi

Equations

It's easier to be fearless
when we remember
that we are deathless.

Yahia Lababidi

Love

Devoted to life of the mind,
he came late to love poetry
— through songs of adoration,
ecstasy and surrender —
address to the divine.

Yahia Lababidi

Biographies

John Allman recently released an 8th book of poetry, *ALGORITHMS* (Quale Press 2012). Other recent poetry books include *LOEW'S TRIBORO* (2004) and *LOWCOUNTRY* (2007), both published by New Directions. New work soon to appear in *THE YALE REVIEW, HOTEL AMERIKA, THE GETTYSBURG REVIEW*. Retired from teaching, Mr. Allman lives in Katonah, NY.

Steve Baldwin was born in the heartland of N. Illinois, but was transplanted to the PNW via Hawaii. He likes to fuse photography with graffiti, nature and poetry. Also, photography with graffiti and T-shirt designs. First novel will be an Urban Fantasy with some aforementioned themes.

Madeleine Beckman is a poet and fiction and nonfiction writer. She is Nonfiction Editor for *IthacaLit,* a literary journal, and a Contributing Reviewer for the *Bellevue Literary Review*. Her work has been published in books, journals, anthologies, and online. She is the recipient of awards and grants, including a Poetry Society of America Award, a New York Foundation for the Arts Award, and a grant from the Irish Arts Council of Ireland. Her poetry collection, *Dead Boyfriends,* was recently reissued by Limoges Press. Madeleine teaches in the Medicine & Humanism Program/NYU Medical School and privately. Her web site is: http://www.writedowntown.com

Kayleigh Brookes is an illustrator and novice poet who resides in The Little Room at House of Brookes (~www.houseofbrookes.com).

Michael Campagnoli taught literature and writing while studying for a Ph.D. at Indiana University. Since then, he has worked a variety of jobs, including fisherman, journalist, and short-order cook. Currently, he proofreads/line-edits the local newspaper and home-schools his sixteen year-old son. His awards have included the New Letters Poetry Award, the All Nations Press Chapbook Award, and The Chiron Review Novella Prize. His fiction and poetry have appeared in *New Letters, Nimrod, Southern Humanities Review, Rosebud, Natural Bridge, Inkwell, Red Rock Review, Crab Creek Review, Emerson Review, Rattle, Palimpsest, Tule, Blue Earth Review, Ellipsis*, and elsewhere.

Chloe N. Clark is a current MFA candidate. Her work has appeared in such places as *Rosebud, Prick of the Spindle, Fogged Clarity*, and more. Follow her on Twitter @PintsNCupcakes.

Kathryn Dyche Dechairo is a mixed media artist and blogger with a passion for nature, texture and poetry. Her creative journey first began during her early thirty's. Barely audible at first, like a soft whisper. It took the death of her father and a move stateside for those initial whisperings to find their voice and become a catalyst for her creativity. Kathryn can now be found in Ohio still listening to those whispers, the ones that gently nudge her forward towards her dreams.

Jane Dougherty writes fiction, fantasy, and historical fantasy. She also writes short stories and poetry. Her first novel is to be released shortly through Musa Publishing. Her roots are very deep, but she has always lived far from home. An attachment to the natural world helps put the melancholy in perspective and give it a focus.

Bill Ellsworth is a 56 year-old amateur artist.

Teresa Evangeline spends her days on a little piece of land along the Pine River observing and experiencing the beauty of the world. Then, through poetry, she distills these moments down to their essence.

Donna Falcone lives in Pennsylvania with her husband, two sons, and a very heavy dog suffering the longstanding delusion that he is a Pomeranian. After devoting 28 years to the field of Early Childhood Education, she now enjoys writing and photographing nature. Donna's poetry, essays, and photographs can be found the Brighter Side Blog, under the tagline "I want my poetry to matter at the bottom line, where the heart sits tight in readiness for something to resonate".

Linda Nemec Foster is the author of nine collections of poetry including *Amber Necklace from Gdansk* (finalist for the Ohio Book Award in Poetry) and *Listen to the Landscape* (short-listed for the Michigan Notable Book Award). Her most recent book, *Talking Diamonds*, was selected by *ForeWord Magazine* as a finalist for their Book of the Year Award in 2010. Her work has also appeared in *The Georgia Review, Nimrod, North American Review, New American Writing, Quarterly West,* and *DoubleTake.* She is the founder of the Contemporary Writers Series at Aquinas College in Grand Rapids, Michigan.

gennepher lives in North Wales,UK. She began writing micropoetry on Twitter as @gennepher a few years ago. Her interest in poetry has been haiku,tanka and haiga.

Bobby Gutierrez is a photographer and glazier from New Mexico. He has previously published in *Gizmodo* and is preparing to begin formal training in photography at the New York Institute of Photography.

Leigh Herrick is an award-winning poet, writer, and recording artist, as well-as a two-time Pushcart Prize nominee. Her recently released e-book is *WITHOUT, HAIKU.* For detailed information regarding all of Herrick's books, recordings, and other art, please visit www.LeighHerrick.com.

Ink is the pseudonym of a Dutch photographer who started writing in order to find the caption to accompany the emotion of his captures. This became a quest in itself. He shares his work on his blog at: www.handpickedmyself.wordpress.com.

Brad Johnson lives in Oakland, California. When he is not working as a bookseller and playing domestic, he tweets up a storm as @AhabLives and quietly blogs at Departure Delayed (http://departuredelayed.wordpress.com).. He should be working more diligently on his first novel.

Bauke Kamstra has been a visual artist for over thirty years, and considers this good training for poetry. He now resides in Nova Scotia, where in the early mornings he continues to listen to what the silence tells him, & translate it into poetry. His poetry has been previous published by *Poetry Nook Magazine* and the *Vine Leaves Journal* (including the "Best of Vine Leaves 2013"). You can find more of his work at on twitter by following @wyrde.

M. Kei is a tall ship sailor and award-winning poet who lives on Maryland's Eastern shore. He is the editor-in-chief of *Take Five: Best Contemporary Tanka*, and the editor of *Atlas Poetica: A Journal of Poetry of Place in Contemporary Tanka*. His most recent collection of poetry is *January, A Tanka Diary* (October, 2013). He is also the author of the award-winning gay *Age of Sail* adventure novels, *Pirates of the Narrow Seas*. He can be followed on Twitter @kujakupoet, or visit AtlasPoetica.org.

Laura Kynch is a poet and ethnographer of the future living in Copenhagen and sometimes in the islands of Orkney, Scotland. She blurs her many labels together as a transdiscplinary writer, weaving together poetry, ethnography, and technology into many forms, from ethnographic prose-poems in academic journals to micropoetry published on Twitter at @laurakynch.

Yahia Lababidi is an Egyptian-American thinker and poet, is the author of 5 books in 4 genres. His latest is "Barely There," a new collection of short poems that touches on the life of the spirit. Lababidi has been featured on NPR, Al Jazeera and in The Guardian, among other places. For more information, please visit: http://amazon.com/author/yahialababidi

"Beez" Laine lives in Australia. She is an artist and also writes poetry. Beez started using the internet three years ago to connect with other artists and writers and shares her works using twitter. She also maintains two blogs msbeez.wordpress.com and beezknez.blogspot.com.au.

Amie McIntyre is an aspiring poet in the field of micro-poetry.

Jane Mellor is a graduate of Simon Fraser University's *The Writer's Studio* in Vancouver, British Columbia, and was host and organizer of TWS Reading Series, a monthly literary event for notable and emerging writers. Published *inQuills* Canadian Poetry Magazine, *emerge*, *TWS* website, *The Toronto Quarterly*, *Leaf Press*, *Contemporary Horizon Magazine*, and *Contemporary Horizon Anthology* in Bucharest, she was also long listed for SFU's 1st Book Competition. *Delicate Availability*, Jane's first book of poetry and prose, is available through most booksellers. She lives in Vancouver.

Richard Moss has been an "active poet" and writer since he was twelve years old, born and raised in Baltimore, Maryland. Never caring much for public or private schools, Richard was basically home schooled, through lively discussions with his father around the family dining table. Richard is an avid reader, of science, history, and literature. Having lived and traveled across the lower forty-eight, Richard chooses never to stray too far from the Rappahannock River or the Chesapeake Bay, nor from his wife, two adult children, grandson and extended family.

Jessica Otto lives in Arkansas with her husband and many cats. Blogs and writes at http://chewingwormwood.blogspot.com.

Jamal Parker is currently a senior at Colonial High School. He was in the Creative Writing Program at Douglas Anderson School of the Arts for three years, and studied in the program at LaVilla School of the Arts as well.

Marianne Paul is a Canadian novelist and poet whose work has appeared in a variety of magazines and anthologies. Her recent books include "Above and Below the Waterline," a poetry collection, and "Tending Memory," a novel. Visit her website at www.mariannepaul.com

Eusebeia Philos was born and raised in Cleveland, Ohio. Poetry and its ability to create an emotional experience from words and ideas has always fascinated him. Many of his long form poems can be found at eusebeiaphilos.blogspot.com. You can also find him sharing micropoetry on Twitter @Eusebeia_Philos. Eusebeia received his B.A. in Philosophy (with a certificate in Bioethics) from Cleveland State University. He currently resides in the rolling farmlands of Northeastern Ohio.

Dr. Jasmine Pradissitto was born in Taunton to an Italian father and French mother, but moved to South London, where she still lives with her teenage son and where her practice is based. Her path to art has not been the usual one. She fell into the sciences, working for ICI for a brief stint, culminating with a Ph. D from UCL in 1996 on the Quantum behaviour of silicon. But she was also attending Goldsmiths College in the evening to study fine art. Like a lost melody that kept resonating in my head, the two worlds just seemed, linked and experimentation both traditional and cutting edge is inherent to my practice. In addition to painting, she then set up a successful, consultancy delivering creative science and thinking to children and teachers and that too, has crossed into her practice.

Diana Raab is an award-winning poet, memoirist, blogger, writing instructor and author of eight books. She has four poetry collections: *Listening to Africa, Dear Anaïs: My Life in Poems for You, The Guilt Gene* and *My Muse Undresses Me*. Her next collection, *Lust* will be released in February 2014. She's a regular blogger on the Huffington Post:
http://www.huffingtonpost.com/diana-m-raab
Her website is www.dianaraab.com.

Dave Read is a Canadian poet living in Calgary, Alberta. His work has previously appeared in Poetry Nook and on the Jar of Stars website. You can find his micro-poetry on Twitter @AsSlimAsImBeing.

John Reinhart is a teacher, a husband, and a father of three. He works his hands into the world in every avenue he can find to demonstrate that loving the world is the foundation of all experience, knowledge, and understanding.

Vipul Rikhi is a writer based in Bangalore, India. He writes poetry, drama, and short and long fiction. His novel '2012 Nights' was published in India late last year by Fingerprint, and a collection of poetry, 'Solitary beyond Time', was published bilingually by the Akademie Schloss Solitude in Germany where He had a fellowship for literature in 2010-2011.

Elisavietta Ritchie's most recent of 17+ books and chapbooks of poetry and fiction are: *Tiger Upstairs on Connecticut Avenue (2013), Feathers, Or, Love on the Wing, (2013); From the Artist's Deathbed 2012; Cormorant Beyond the Compost, Awaiting Permission to Land, and Real Toads. Tightening The Circle Over Eel Country* won Great Lakes Colleges Association's "New Writer's Award"; *Raking The Snow and In Haste I Write You This Note: Stories & Half-Stories* Washington Writers' Publishing House winners; *"Camille Pissarro's THE BATHER Speaks"* won *The Ledge* 2011 poetry award; Work in many publications and anthologies (including *Poetry, Sound and Sense; The 90th Anniversary Poetry Anthology; When I'm An Old Woman I Shall Wear Purple*, etc).

Fernanda Rocha is a Brazilian journalist and writer. She was born in the state of Santa Catarina (South of Brazil). She uses the name Fereh Rocha as a writer and is someone who has always loved art in general. Fereh enjoys music very much, traveling, meeting new people and is a big fan of cinema. She prefers stories and poems to news on newspapers. She shares her work on her blog (www.fereh.wordpress.com) about poetry and music, fan page (www.facebook.com/BlogdaFereh) and Twitter account (@blogdafereh). This year Fereh wrote some lyrics to different Brazilian musicians. One of the songs was recorded and can be found on SoundCloud (www.soundcloud.com/ferehrocha)

Michael Seese is an information security professional by day. Or, as his son could say even at age three, "Daddy keeps people's money safe." He has published four books: *The Secret World Of Gustave Eiffel, Haunting Valley, Scrappy Business Contingency Planning*, and *Scrappy Information Security*, not to mention a lot of flash fiction, short stories, and poems. Other than that, he spends his spare time rasslin' with three young'uns.
Visit www.MichaelSeese.com to laugh with him or at him.

Steve Shultz is a poet and journalist from Aurora, Colorado. Steve lives in the Mile High City suburb with his wife and two children. His poetry has been published online in a variety of publications, and in print in two anthologies, most recently in the *The dVerse Anthology*. His first book of poetry, *FM Ghost*, was released in April of 2013 via ALL CAPS PUBLISHING, an indie poetry and fiction collective based out of Massachusetts. You can sample more of his writing at http://fmghost.wordpress.com.

Anupam Sinha is a computational biologist working at the Centre for DNA Fingerprinting and Diagnostics, Hyderabad, India. Apart from his interest in science, he also loves literature.

Chris Smith is a dreamer, writer, photographer, and artist who lives every day with one goal, to express herself and grow. She's working on her fourth 365 Photo Project, and in January 2013 completed a Photo Project following her Mom through Stage 3 Cancer. Chris writes in a variety of genres, from nonfiction to erotica. She's hammering out three books, and pondering a padded dish room. Find her on Twitter: @RantingsOfaGirl. Read her on Wattpad:http://www.wattpad.com/user/ChrisRantingsOfaGirl

Debbie Strange is a member of the Writers' Collective of Manitoba and the United Haiku and Tanka Society. Her writing and photography has received awards, and her work has been published in print and online in several journals. Words are the source of Debbie's solace and salvation. She can be found on twitter @Debbie_Strange

Emily Strauss has an M.A. in English, but is self-taught in poetry. Over 120 of her poems appear in dozens of online venues and in anthologies. The natural world is generally her framework; she often focuses on the tension between nature and humanity, using concrete images to illuminate the loss of meaning between them. She is a semi-retired teacher living in California.

Cletis L Stump lives amid the beautiful Appalachians and he keeps his eyes open. He is the co administrator of the micropoetry tumblr Late Night Footfalls.

Fabiyas M V is a writer from Orumanayur village in Kerala, India. He is the author of Moonlight and Solitude. His fiction and poems have appeared in *Literary The Hatchet, Words With Jam, E Fiction, Selected Poems 2012 by Pendle War Poetry, Inspired By Tagore, ACWC Anthology, Indian Ink, Animal Antics 2012,* and in several anthologies by Forward Poetry and other publishers in India and abroad. He won the Poetry Soup International Award , USA in 2011 and 2012, a prize by the British Council in 2011, the RSPCA Pet Poetry Contest, UK in 2012, the Whistle Press Poetry Prize, India in 2012 and a sponsor's prize in Eriata Oribhaba Poetry Competition, Nigeria in 2013. He took honourable mention in Political Poet Poetry Competition , USA in 2013. He was the finalist for Mattia International Poetry Contest , Canada in 2011 and 2012. All India Radio had broadcast his poems.

Frank Watson was born in Venice, California and now lives in New York City. He enjoys literature, art, calligraphy, history, jazz, international culture, and travel. His books include *Fragments: poetry, ancient & modern* (editor), *One Hundred Leaves: a new, annotated translation of the* Hyakunin Isshu (editor and translator), and *The dVerse Anthology: Voices of Contemporary World Poetry* (editor). He is also editor of the monthly journal of poetry and art, *Poetry Nook*. His work has appeared in *Rosebud, Bora,* and *Prune Juice* literary journals and will appear in the upcoming *Tarot Poetry* anthology, *Bright Stars* anthology, and *Atlas Poetica 17* literary journal. Frank shares his work on his poetry blog (www.followtheblueflute.com) and his Twitter account (@FollowBlueFlute).

Credits

An earlier version of "Tea-Time with Babushka, Aged Ninety-Four" appeared in *Southern Poetry Review*; reprinted in *Tightening The Circle Over Eel Country*, Acropolis Books, © 1974 Elisavietta Ritchie.

Yahia Lababidi's poems were published in his book, *Barely There*, and are copyright © 2013 by Yahia Lababidi.

Linda Nemec Foster's poem, "The Field Behind the Dying Father's House," was previously published in her book *Talking Diamonds* (New Issues Press, 2009). Copyright 2009 by Linda Nemec Foster.

www.ingramcontent.com/pod-product-compliance
Lightning Source LLC
LaVergne TN
LVHW051010080826
845145LV00009B/2545

* 9 7 8 1 9 3 9 8 3 2 0 6 1 *